THE SCENE STEALER

The Heart of a Worshipper
Always Gets God's Attention

THE SCENE STEALER

The Heart of a Worshipper
Always Gets God's Attention

GARY HAWKINS, SR.

HIGHLAND PARK, ILLINOIS

THE SCENE STEALER
The Heart of a Worshipper Always Gets God's Attention
by
Gary Hawkins, Sr.

Printed in the United States of America

Published By
Mall Publishing Company
641 Homewood Avenue
Highland Park, Illinois 60035
877-203-2453

Cover Design by Quiana Clark

Interior Layout and Design by
Faith Instructional Design
551 Mountain Park Trail
Stone Mountain, GA 30087
770-498-6700

ISBN 1-934165-07-7

Unless otherwise noted, all Scripture quotations are taken from the King James Version of the Holy Bible.

For licensing or copyright information, please contact:

Gary Hawkins Ministries
P.O. Box 870989
Stone Mountain, GA 30087
Phone: 800-821-6156 Fax: 678-510-1333
vof@voicesfaith.org • www.voicesfaith.org

DEDICATION

❖ ❖ ❖

For over twelve years, I have pastored Voices of Faith Ministries in Stone Mountain, Georgia and recently a second location in Conyers, Georgia. No matter where I travel, I always brag about my congregation. Yes, I have the best congregation in the universe! Therefore, I pause and praise God for sending them to me.

Thanks to the Voices of Faith family for believing in what God has entrusted to me. You were created with a purpose, and you made it easy to teach the Word which is now birthed into this book. Thank you and from the bottom of my heart, I love you!

Finally, to those scene stealers who strive to get God's attention by any means necessary. May God free you of your surroundings so you can praise Him in the grocery store, in the middle of rush hour traffic, or even during a ballet.

❖ ❖ ❖

ACKNOWLEDGEMENTS

❖ ❖ ❖

To my God, there is none other like You—no not one. I love You! Thank You for entrusting me with another assignment. Thank You for your unwavering grace and mercy shown towards me despite my handicaps. I praise You!

To my beautiful wife, Debbie Elaine Hawkins, you are like the dew drops in the morning. There is freshness from you each and every day. Thank you for believing in me, and thank you for pushing me!

To my four wonderful children—Elaina, Ashley, Gary Jr., and Kalen—I am breathless without you in my life! My world revolves around yours. Thank you for unselfishly sharing me with others.

To my sweet mom, Mary Louise Robertson, my love for you is unconditional. I am walking in destiny because of you. Don't stop praying for me and my family. It is working! God is answering your prayers.

To my mother-in-love, Elzina Owens, your love has caused me to be too blessed to be stressed! I am the most blessed son-in-love in the world.

I wish to especially thank Angia Levels. Favor is now in your house! Now is the time to begin experiencing God's manifestation.

Quiana Clark, God has shifted you to a new dimension. Your focus in the kingdom is unbelievable!

To my brother and sister-in-love, Aaron and Mia Hawkins, thank you for ALWAYS being there for my family! I cannot count the number of times we needed you to pull us out of a difficult situation and you did. I love you!

To the rest of my family—Walter, John, Reginald, Denita, Wayne, Aldreamer, Mary, Warren, Victorina, Chris, Theresa, Gladys, Ann, Gail, Shelia, Dwight, Andrea, Michael, Roy, and Judy—God could not have sent a more loving family. Not a day passes by that you are not on my mind. I often pray for your safety as well as prosperity in your life.

To Earl, Jasper, Paula, and Theresa, thank you for accepting me just as I am. I am always praying that God will open windows of heaven and pour out blessings that you cannot contain.

To my nieces, nephews, cousins, and friends (too many to name), I love you and appreciate your love and prayers.

To my pastoral staff—Lorraine Dykes, Tyrone Lane, Barbara Jones, James and Valerie Murkison, Althea Brooks, Lakisha Chatman, Neva Romaine, Cynthia Ward, David Ferebee, Dwaine Johnson, Zenda Duren, Laura Walker, Shawnea Barry, Taronda Hall, Bernie Grant, Debra Adams, Dexter Hall, Nikki Washington, Michael Dupree, Chris Jackson, Charles Ford, and Paulette Ruiz—this ministry would not be successful without your dedication and commitment. Thank you for helping to advance the kingdom. I love each of you beyond measure.

TABLE OF CONTENTS

Introduction

Ever since my childhood, I have always been intrigued with movies. My favorites were the Bruce Lee movies. My friends and I pretended to know martial arts and acted out each scene. Now that I am a husband and father, my favorite pastime is going to the movies with my wife and children.

I always make sure I am there for the previews. Typically, the director will show a glimpse of some of the best scenes of the upcoming picture with the leading stars to capture your interest and persuade you to see the movie. What amazes me is when the movie finally premieres, some unknown actor often steals the scene. Your attention is no longer on the leading actor, but on a sole character who completely diverts your interest by the way they played a simple scene or said a single line. It is like the supporting actor said, "I only have this one time to get noticed and right now I don't have anything to lose. I'm going to give it my best shot." Some of the most well-known actors today got their big breaks by being a scene stealer.

In the Christian life, a scene stealer is a person who has exhausted every avenue (doctor, psychic, self-help). It is a person who realizes he or she has nothing to lose by trusting Jesus. A scene stealer is desperate, obnoxious, and persistent. A scene stealer is not concerned about being embarrassed, and does not care who's watching.

The prerequisite for becoming a scene stealer is faith.

> *But without faith it is impossible to please Him: for he that cometh to God must believe that He is, and that He is a rewarder of them that diligently seek Him (Hebrews 11:6).*

You cannot be a scene stealer if you do not believe that God is who He says He is. Why would you waste your time on your knees if you didn't believe the prayer you just prayed could be answered? Oftentimes, as Christians, we don't feel we deserve miracles in our lives. Too many times, we become professional lookers—watching everyone else receive blessings while wondering, "How do I get blessed? What do I need to do?"

When are you going to become a scene stealer? When are you going to say, "I am sick and tired of being sick and tired?" Perhaps, you're okay with your current situation and have no desire to do anything different, or maybe, just maybe, you want things to change, and you don't know how to go about it. Maybe you have been battling with the same issues for a number of years and your frustration has gotten the best of you.

Can I share a secret with you? You're not alone. This book was spiritually revealed to me as a result of my becoming a scene stealer. If you're ready for a change and desire the very best for your life, I encourage you to continue reading as I introduce you to some ridiculously outstanding scene stealers.

Scene stealers are not looking to be entertained; nor do they have foolishness on their minds. They come to church expecting a miracle.

Scene 1

Two Blind Men

Have you ever personally met anyone who was born blind? This person never had the opportunity to see the world as you and I. They were not afforded the opportunity to say, "My, how beautiful the sun looks in the evening just before dusk," or "How beautiful the stars look surrounding the half shaped moon!" Those of us who can see often take sight for granted. The person without the ability to see may ask someone blessed with vision, "Tell me how beautiful the sun looks, or describe the moon and the stars." Depending on their creativity, people with sight usually describe the scene as if they were painting a picture.

The Book of Matthew describes two blind men. Obviously, neither could paint a picture for the other since both were blind. These two men desperately wanted to see.

Matthew 9:26 says, *"And the fame hereof went abroad into all that land."* The fame was the word of mouth of the miracles Jesus was performing. The people heard about Him, and His fame grew throughout the region. Great crowds began to follow Him.

What will make you stand out from the crowd? What will cause you to become a scene stealer? Matthew 9:27 says, *"And when Jesus departed thence, two blind men **followed** Him, **crying** and **saying**, Thou son of David, have **mercy** on us."* The two blind men could not see the miracles being performed for they were without physical sight, but someone painted a picture of Jesus and all that He was doing—such a picture that the two blind men followed Him. Their abilities to hear and speak were not challenged for they heard who Jesus was and referred to Him as, *"Thou son of David."* Certainly, their ability to walk was not challenged; for the Bible said they followed Jesus. Lastly, their ability to think was not an issue as they knew exactly what they needed—mercy.

As simple as their request seemed, the two blind men faced challenges that could have easily caused them to remain in the same position. They could have grown weary and simply discouraged one another saying, "I've been blind so long that I'm used to being blind. If I see, I see. If I don't, oh well." This is usually the comment made by most Christians. We don't believe that a miracle could happen to us. We don't believe that God wants to bless us so we make excuses to justify our current state of being.

Instead of speaking negatively, the two blind men shared each others infirmities. Their state of being was the same. They both desperately wanted to see, and neither was embarrassed to do whatever it took to make it happen.

Let's take a look at where Jesus was and how these two blind men positioned themselves for their miracle. Prior to these scene stealers [the two blind men] there were other scene stealers in the course of events that led to their encounter with Jesus. In the midst of Jesus ministering to His disciples, a certain ruler, Jairus, came and worshiped Him and told Jesus that his daughter was dead at home. Jairus believed that if Jesus would come and lay hands upon her she would live. Jesus and His disciples arose and followed Jairus.

Remember, Matthew 9:26 says, *"And the fame hereof went abroad into all that land."* The word was out about Jesus and who He was. There were more than just the disciples traveling with Him. Imagine the Macy's Thanksgiving Day Parade. There are people who are actually a part of the parade, and then there are spectators who stand on the side of the road. Thousands of people go to the Macy's parade. The parade is so huge that people plan a year in advance to attend. That's how it was the day the blind men met Jesus. There was a parade of people following Jesus as He followed Jairus.

Now, Jesus was traveling to perform a miracle at Jairus' house, but in the midst of His travel, a certain woman [another scene stealer] who was stricken with an issue of blood touched Him. There was a crowd; yet, this scene stealer said, "I know You're heading to perform another miracle, but just keep on walking. All I need to do is just touch the hem of Your garment."

Too many times we beat around the bush about what we need God to do for our lives. God already knows what you need. He just wants you to open your mouth and ask.

This scene stealer's belief was so strong that as she touched Jesus, He paused and asked, *"Who touched me?" (Luke 8:45).* Keep in mind there was a multitude of people and any number of people could have touched Him, but Jesus knew this was a touch like none other. Her touch (faith) was so strong it drew virtue from Jesus.

Can you imagine the thoughts that were running through Jairus' mind as he looked on impatiently? He must have thought to himself (if not aloud), "What do you mean who touched you? Who cares?" What a great example that shows our time is not God's time! Jesus knew how much time He needed to perform the miracle of Jairus' daughter. As harsh as it seemed to Jairus, Jesus knew his daughter was not dead, just asleep.

This woman, this scene stealer, was so desperate she could not wait until Jesus returned from Jairus' house. She couldn't take a chance on Him taking another route and having to wait for her opportunity to come again. This scene stealer did not possess a spirit of procrastination. She was far too desperate to wait.

Procrastination has become a part of our daily living. We say things like, "Oh, I'll get to know Jesus tomorrow," or "I'll join church next Sunday," or "I'll call my mom next week," or "I'll start that business next year." Quit putting off tomorrow what you can do today. Denounce procrastination right now. In the name of Jesus, denounce it!

Jesus turned to the woman and said *"Daughter, be of good comfort; thy faith hath made thee whole" (Matthew 9:22)*. Her desperation caused her to act and her faith in Jesus brought her healing.

Meanwhile, Jairus waited on Jesus to continue the journey to his house. After all, his daughter was lying home dead, and he just needed Jesus to get to his house. Jesus departed for Jairus' house, and the two blind men followed Him. Jesus heard the blind men calling out to Him, but continued walking. Wait a minute! Are you telling me that *our* Jesus kept walking? Yes! Even though He heard the two blind men, Jesus continued walking and entered into Jairus' house. The two blind men continued following Him. They had heard of the miracles He had performed, and they had just heard Him heal the scene stealer with the issue of blood. They were two desperate blind men, and they knew what they wanted!

What did I say about the characteristics of scene stealers? They are never embarrassed. When you have something on your mind that you need God to do, you cannot be embarrassed by who is around you. You cannot worry about church folk. Sometimes you may be the only one shouting or the only one running. You will do it because no one else understands what you have gone through. They don't know what your "Hallelujah!" means to you.

These two blind men didn't care about what other people thought about them. They cried out loud, although Jesus kept walking. Why would Jesus keep walking with two blind men calling out? Do you think Jesus should have shown pity? Don't let what looks like a lack of response from Jesus cause you to miss the blessing. You have to understand that a scene stealer has tough skin. You cannot be a sensitive person and also be a scene stealer. Those two do not go hand-in-hand. That's like oil and water—they don't mix. You just can't put them together.

A scene stealer cannot be a sensitive person crying, "Oh, you hurt my feelings." Scene stealers have hard, tough skin. They know what people are saying about them, but they don't care. They can still smile in the midst of adversity because they have faith that God will do what He said.

Jesus kept walking, knowing very well these men were blind and physically challenged. They kept yelling, and He kept walking. There are a lot of people who "get their praise on," but everybody who is "getting their praise on" is not as serious as they may seem to be. Some people come to church just to see what "Sister So-and-So" is wearing while others wake up with Jesus on their minds and come to church with expectancy. Scene stealers are not looking to be entertained; nor do they have foolishness on their minds. They come to church expecting a miracle.

For example, those who shout in church. How do we know which ones are scene stealers? A scene stealer doesn't stop shouting! When everybody else sits down, a scene stealer is still up shouting and praising God. A scene stealer says, "Pastor, I know you told me to go back to my seat and sit down, but God's been too good to me. Can I give one last praise? Can I give God the best I can give Him? I know you told me time was up, but you don't know what I've been through! I've got to praise Him just a little while longer!" Scene stealers have to keep on praising God because they have been through too much, and they just can't stop their praise like that. They have to give God continual praise.

Jesus continued walking away from the two blind men, because He wanted to see if they truly had faith.

Hebrews 11:6 says, *"Without faith it is impossible to please Him."* It does not say *without praise* or *without prayer,* but *without faith,* you cannot please God. By Jesus walking away, He was able to determine whether they really believed He could do what they were asking.

Our little faith and carnal minds would have said, "Ah forget that, I'm not chasing behind Him. He heard me the first time. I don't care who He is. By the way, who *does* He think He is anyway?" Attitudes set in, and all it takes is one person in the crowd to become negative to justify your negative thoughts. "Ah, that girl wasn't sick. That girl was already healed. He just *said* He healed her. That woman's blood had dried up the day before she touched Him." We will justify anything that doesn't make sense to us just to make us feel good.

When Jesus didn't stop, they said, *"Thou son of David" (Matthew 9:27).* Scene stealers always know who they worship. Hebrews 11:6 continues, *"......for he that cometh to God must believe that He is, and that He is a rewarder of them that diligently seek Him."* You have to know that the person you're going to, and making yourself look like a fool over, is someone who can deal with your situation. God is the only one who can change your circumstances.

Scene stealers never rely on Mama's prayers. They go to God on their own behalf. You can't go on behalf of somebody else when you have something you need

God to do in your life. You have to go for yourself. All Jesus wants to know is do you believe? How bad do you want it (sight, career, spouse, home)? Do you really know Me for yourself, or are you repeating what you heard someone else say?

Matthew 9:28 says, *"And when He was come into the house, the blind men came to Him."* Wait a second, are you telling me that these two blind men went into another man's house? They were blind. How did they even know which way Jesus went? The blind men were scene stealers. Scene stealers ask questions. "Hey, which house did Jesus go in? If you can just point me to the house and get me into the yard, I'll find a way to get into the house."

Scene stealers are desperate and crazy. When scene stealers have something on their minds, they will get crazy before Jesus. They don't ask if anyone is at home. They'll say, "Look, I heard that Jesus was in this house. I need to speak to Him. Can you get Him out here in a hurry?"

Look at what Jesus said to them: *"Believe ye that I am able to do this? They said unto him, Yea, Lord"* (*Matthew 9:28*). Now, if the two blind men had made it all the way into Jairus' house, why would Jesus have to ask them if they believe? Because you have to believe He can do what you ask. You can't go all the way to His house, do all that struggling and don't believe. When Jesus asked the two blind men if they believed that he was able to give them sight, they did not stutter or stumble. They said together, "Yes, Lord" (Matthew 9:28).

These men were two desperate people hanging with each other. They encouraged each other. They were in the same situation; they both wanted to see. They are an example for us. We have to be with people who have been *battle-tested*. We have to be with people who have no doubt that God will do what He said He will do. We have to get around some encouragers and sometimes around a bunch of misfits who know that God can bring them out of any situation.

Matthew 9:29 says, *"Then touched he their eyes, saying, According to your faith be it unto you."* Why would Jesus touch their eyes? Why wouldn't He just speak to them and say, "Go, your faith has made thee whole?" He told the woman with the issue of blood, *"Thy faith hath made thee whole"* (Matthew 9:22). Why would He have to touch their eyes? What were they using their faith for? What were they pursuing Him for? Their sight! They had faith Jesus could make them see, so He only touched them in the area where they had exercised their faith.

Always pray specifically for what you desire from God. When you pray specifically, that's where you will apply your faith. The reason our prayers are not answered is because we do not pray specifically with faith. Their eyes needed healing, so He touched them where their faith was.

After He touched their eyes, the verse continues saying, *"according to your faith."* Where was their faith? It was resting where they wanted the healing. Too many of us pray general prayers, and God doesn't touch us because we have not been specific. If you're going to get a breakthrough from God, you have to be specific in what you ask God to do. He will then be specific in where He heals and delivers you. If your finances need healing, then ask Him to touch your wallet, purse, or bank account. You cannot pray a general prayer because you will never know if God answered it. We have to learn how to pray about what's bothering us.

Jesus touched them where their faith was.

> *Believe ye that I am able to do this? They said unto him, Yea, Lord. Then touched he their eyes, saying, According to your faith be it unto you. And their eyes were opened; and Jesus straightly charged them, saying, See that no man know it (Matthew 9:28–30).*

Have you ever received a blessing and tried to keep it to yourself? These two men had been blind all their lives. Jesus healed them and said, "Now, go and don't tell a single person." They said "Yeah, okay, thank you Jesus. *"But they, when they were departed, spread abroad his fame in all that country"* (Matthew 9:31). As soon as they left His sight, they started telling everybody in arms length. Not only did they tell, notice what they did: *"As they went out, behold, they brought to him a dumb man possessed with a devil" (Matthew 9:32).* These two blind men stole the scene twice. After they were healed, they found somebody else who needed to be healed. I can hear them telling the dumb man, "Boy get yourself over here! You don't have to stay in the condition you're in. We know somebody who can heal you right now." They had become a battle-tested people.

The two blind men already stood out because of what they did in the crowd. Then, they left the crowd, found a dumb man and brought him back to Jesus to be healed. These two desperate men who were no longer blind got in front of the crowd for another healing. All their lives they had been blind. They could have selfishly hid their miracle, but instead they shared the good news. It took some crazy scene stealers to understand how to get a blessing, and then bring another person to Jesus.

Matthew 9:32–33 says, *"As they went out, behold, they brought to him a dumb man possessed with a devil. And when the devil was cast out, the dumb spake."* Why didn't Jesus test this man's faith? Why didn't He use sign language to find out whether he believed? He tested the blind men, but He didn't do that to this man. If Jesus had wanted to question him, He could have. When you have been battled-tested, God doesn't have to ask you questions anymore.

The blind men had already proven their faith. It wasn't even about the dumb man; God was still honoring the faith of the blind men. After God had tested the blind, He didn't need to test the dumb man. Instead, God said, "I don't need to test you again. I know you're with Me. I know you trust Me. So if you're bringing somebody else for Me to heal, I'm just going to bless him just because he's associated with you. I'm going to bless him just because he's in good company. I'm going to bless him just because you've been praying, praising, and worshipping Me."

Who are you hanging around? In the Old Testament, King David blessed Mephibosheth's servant, Ziba, just because he was associated with Mephibosheth (2 Samuel 9). It had nothing to do with him. You need to be with people who have experienced God. Get around people who know without a shadow of a doubt what God has done, and what He is going to do for them. When they bring you to the altar, it's not about you. God will say, I sent you through the fire and the fire has made you pure gold. It strengthened you. It was the struggle that did this.

Matthew 9:33 continues saying, *"The multitudes marvelled, saying, It was never so seen in Israel."* In other words, they had not seen anything like this in all of the church, and the church people said, "We haven't seen anyone this desperate."

Scene stealers do not care about other people's points of view because they are desperate to get something from God. Scene stealers know there is no such thing as "coincidence" in the body of Christ. Anytime you find that your back is up against the wall and a miracle occurs, you have to believe and thank God for the miracle. The moment you believe is the moment your faith actually kicks in for God to give the blessing. You may think it was a coincidence that God showed up at the midnight hour, but it wasn't until the midnight hour that your faith got strong enough that God said, "Now, I will honor your faith." At the midnight hour you became desperate for God, and He honored your prayer in the same midnight hour. The Bible says God inhabits the praises of His people. The word inhabit means "He comes and lives with you." He comes and stays with you the moment you open your mouth and praise Him.

Blind Bartimaeus was another scene stealer who was screaming by the pool of Bethesda. His screams were actually a form of praise, and he stole the scene. God stopped and blessed Bartimaeus because of his praise. You have to learn how to open your mouth and praise God in the midst of your prayer request, in the midst of your struggle, and in the midst of waiting to be blessed.

What would happen if you acted like you needed a desperate miracle from God every day? From the time you wake up until you go to bed, your assigned angel would never leave your post. It would cause God to say, "She's desperate again. I have to give her what she needs. I have to give her the desires of her heart." When we have that attitude, we will always steal the scene.

If you are going to be a scene stealer, you have to understand there will always be a crowd. There will always be distractions and excuses. You have to find a way to separate yourself from the crowd. You have to let God know that you are desperate, and if anyone is going to be blessed today, it should be you.

Scene One Review

1. What does the word *fame* mean in Matthew 9:26?

2. List the scene stealers who are presented in this chapter.

3. What caused the blind men to be healed?

4. What are characteristics of scene stealers?

5. What is one reason that our prayers are not answered?

Suggested answers to these questions are on page 68.

Scene stealers can be obnoxious. They can be loud and boisterous. They are not embarrassed to stand out in a crowd. Their mission is to do all they can to have God's attention rest upon them.

Scene 2

Blind Bartimaeus

And they came to Jericho: and as he went out of Jericho with his disciples and a great number of people, blind Bartimaeus, the son of Timaeus, sat by the highway side begging. And when he heard that it was Jesus of Nazareth, he began to cry out, and say, Jesus, thou son of David, have mercy on me (Mark 10:46–47).

Scene stealers can be obnoxious. They can be loud and boisterous. They are not embarrassed to stand out in a crowd. Their mission is to do all they can to have God's attention rest upon them. The scene stealer knows that there is always a crowd after God's attention so they do whatever is necessary to separate themselves from the crowd.

What we do to separate ourselves from the crowd is very critical. Blind Bartimaeus understood this and had no problem separating himself from the crowd that was following Jesus. When we read our focal Scripture, there are three significant things that made Bartimaeus a successful scene stealer.

First, Bartimaeus positioned himself to see Jesus. A lot of us miss the hand of God because we place ourselves out of position to receive the blessings that are upon our lives. We were not at the right place at the right time so we mess up our ministry and our blessing because we were out of position.

When Bartimaeus heard Jesus of Nazareth was passing by, he did not ask any questions. He did not ask how many are walking with Him or if He was in a hurry. That was not his concern. His only concern was that he needed a blessing and he needed it right away.

Bartimaeus cried out, *"And when he heard that it was Jesus of Nazareth, he began to cry out, and say, Jesus, thou son of David, have mercy on me" (Mark 10:47).* In other words, he began shouting praises to God aloud.

When we praise God aloud, it causes God to not only hear us, but to also see us and come deal with our situation. "Mercy on me" is translated in the Amplified version of the Bible as, *"Have mercy on me right now."* It is written in the past tense as in *"have mercy on me yesterday."* Bartimaeus wanted Jesus to know that his need was so imperative that He needed the blessing yesterday.

When Bartimaeus began to praise God, he stole the scene. Since there is always a crowd, you have to find a way to do something unique to set you apart from the crowd so God will understand that you are serious about what you need from Him.

The second thing we should notice about Bartimaeus is he was blind. Notice that the writers of the Book of Matthew and the Book of Luke did not feel it necessary to mention Bartimaeus' name. They referred to him as "the blind man." But for some reason, Mark felt it important to call Bartimaeus by name. Mark even went a little further and found out how Bartimaeus became blind. Mark made sure we understood Bartimaeus' condition and desperation. He described him as *"blind Bartimaeus, thou son of Timaeus" (Mark 10:46)*. Bartimaeus' father was blind, and Bartimaeus was *born* blind, which meant he had no one to help him or to encourage him to overcome his situation.

The third thing we should notice about Bartimaeus is that he was poor. He made his living sitting on the side of the road begging for money. Bartimaeus was poor, but he did not ask Jesus for money. He asked Him for mercy.

When Bartimaeus started shaking things up, *"And many charged him that he should hold his peace" (Mark 10:48)*. They warned, threatened, and reprimanded him saying, "Hold your peace! The Master has a lot on His mind, and He doesn't need you bothering Him. If you don't shut up, we're going to hurt you."

Have you ever been in a situation where you needed something so desperately that threats didn't bother you? Have you needed something so badly that name calling didn't hurt you? If you are in a situation where you are down on your luck and don't know how you were going to make it, you cannot let church folk stop you from praising and magnifying God. Why? They don't know your testimony. Churck folk don't know what you are going through from Monday through Saturday. They don't know what happened to you since last Sunday. They have no idea why you are giving God the best praise you can give Him.

Bartimaeus did not let the church folk bother him. He said, "Take a number! You can just get in line to beat me because I'm going to act like a fool as long as Christ is here." The Bible says they shut up, but they didn't understand Bartimaeus. Bartimaeus knew their trying to stop him simply meant the devil did not want him to get what God had for him. So he opened his mouth anyway.

Now, everyone is gifted in different areas. Everybody doesn't have a loud voice. If your voice is light and quiet so you can't yell, that's okay. You can compensate for the weakness of your voice through another area where you are gifted. Bartimaeus couldn't see, but God gave him a loud mouth, so he got God's attention by compensating for his eyesight with his voice. Zacchaeus was too short to see over the crowd, so he compensated for his height by climbing a Sycamore tree to make sure he could see Christ.

You have to give God the best praise you can give Him. Can you do it? For the next thirty seconds, give Him the best you can. If you can't yell, then dance. If you can't dance, then run. If you can't run, then jump. It doesn't matter what you do; just give God your best praise. This is your time for a breakthrough. This is your time to shout. Give God your very best praise.

Have you ever gotten happy on your own praise? Have you ever started praising God and it felt so good that you praised God louder? Sometimes you can shout yourself happy. Sometimes you can make yourself feel good because your praise increases your faith. Keep giving God glory and watch your faith increase. Keep giving God the best praise you can give Him. It will increase your faith because your praise tells God, "I got it Lord! I know who you are Lord. I know you can make a way out of no way, Lord." Your breakthrough is in your praise. Your new house is in your praise. That bill getting paid is in your praise. Every time you praise God, it gives you more confidence.

When you praise God, and people tell you to shut up, know that God is about to do something incredible in your life. Every time you lift up the name of Jesus and the people around you knock you over, it's time to increase your praise. Whatever you gave God earlier, give Him more, and then watch your faith increase.

You must know why you praise God. Paul says in 1 Corinthians 12:3:

> *Wherefore I give you to understand, that no man speaking by the Spirit of God calleth Jesus accursed: and that no man can say that Jesus is the Lord, but by the Holy Ghost.*

In other words, the only way you are going to praise God is because the Holy Spirit revealed to you who He is. Praise God because He is the head of your life. Praise Him because He is King of Kings and Lord of Lords. You know He can make a way out of no way. You know He is a leaning post in the times of trouble. You know He is a life jacket when you are about to drown. That's why you praise Him! Don't praise Him because everybody else is doing it. Praise Him because the Holy Spirit has shown you that there is nobody like Jesus. That's why you praise God!

When I think about the goodness of God and all He has done for me, everything He has brought to me, it makes me want to shout. It makes me want to praise God. It makes me want to lose myself because I know God is real.

Matthew 11:12 says, *"The Kingdom of Heaven suffereth violence, and the violent take it by force."*

Bartimaeus understood there was going to be opposition. As they hit him, he hit them back. As they pushed him, he pushed them back. You have to be willing to take what God wants to give you by force because the devil will try to knock you out. You cannot hesitate. You have to move when things are happening.

Mark 10:49 says that when Bartimaeus got louder, Jesus stood still. Now you know that had to be some crazy praise to cause the Lord to stand still. Jesus was on His way to Jerusalem. He was going to Calvary to redeem us. He did not have anything else on His mind, but Bartimaeus was crazy enough to stop Him along the way.

Restoring Bartimaeus' sight is the very last miracle recorded in the book of Mark. If Bartimaeus had not acted like a fool, Mark's gospel would have reported the last miracle as the healing of the demon-possessed boy (Mark 9:14–29). When your breakthrough comes, move. It may be the last time God moves in your life this way. What would have happened if blind Bartimaeus had said, "This is a path He always takes. I'll wait until next Sunday to shout"?

Are you going to wait to praise God because you just got your hair permed? Are you going to wait to shout because you're wearing a new suit? You may be thinking I can't afford to mess up my hair or ruin my suit, but guess what? Jesus is passing your way. If you want to receive your yesterday blessing today, you had better become a scene stealer like Bartimaeus. Bartimaeus got his breakthrough. The same people who threatened him patted him on the back.

Notice in Mark 10:50, when Jesus called him, Bartimaeus cast off his garment. He cast off the very garment that kept him warm, the very garment that he used for a cushion when sitting on the side of the road begging. When Jesus called him, Bartimaeus got rid of the stuff in his life that was dead weight.

If God is calling you, get rid of any dead weight in your life. There are some people you can walk with, but there are very few people you can pray with. Everybody cannot go to war with you. Everybody has not been battle-tested. Everybody has not gone through the fire. God wants you to get rid of anything that is hindering your walk. Aren't you sick and tired of being sick and tired? Are you ready for a yesterday blessing?

There are very few people who are desperate enough to stand out in a crowd. Scene stealers lay everything on the altar. They give God their best praise. Are you a scene stealer? Then give God the best praise you can. Worship Him like you already have your blessing.

Scene Two Review

1. What is a scene stealer's mission?

2. What three significant things made Bartimaeus a successful scene stealer?

3. What did Bartimaeus ask for?

4. Why do you need to be willing to take what God wants to give you by force?

5. What did Bartimaeus do when Jesus called him? Explain.

Suggested answers to these questions are on page 68.

If you are going to be a scene stealer, let go of your past, speak God's Word over your life, and then lift up your hands to give God the best praise you can.

Scene 3

The Woman With Infirmities

And he was teaching in one of the synagogues on the sabbath. And, behold, there was a woman which had a spirit of infirmity eighteen years, and was bowed together, and could in no wise lift up herself. And when Jesus saw her, he called her to him, and said unto her, Woman, thou art loosed from thine infirmity. And he laid his hands on her: and immediately she was made straight, and glorified God (Luke 13:10–13).

Have you ever been in a deep conversation, when you looked up and saw someone who actually made you forget what you were saying? Jesus was speaking to the congregation (there's the crowd) when He noticed a crippled woman who had been bent over for eighteen years. She was bent over so badly that she could not lift herself up. Jesus understood her problem was not her physical condition. Her problem was that she had become bitter, depressed, and sick because of what people had said about her.

I've been at a point in my life where I was so stressed that it made me physically sick. We have to remember the devil's job is to steal, kill, and destroy. When the devil gets you to the point where he feels like he is breaking you, that is when he jumps on you harder to make you feel worse than you really are. You tell your doctor you are not really feeling well. The doctor takes test after test, but does not find anything because there is nothing physically wrong with you. It is just that you will not let go of yesterday's news.

Some of you are like this woman. Your problem is not really your current situation. Your problem is stuff you won't let go of from your past. Your problem is not with your boss. It is with the boss on your last job. The problem is not with your current husband. You are still dealing with your first husband. The problem is not your current wife; it is what your first wife did to you before you met your new one. You are still stuck on yesterday, and God is trying to bring you into today so He can bless you. Somebody hurt you in the past and you have allowed it to ruin your future. But you have to let go and let God move so He can have

His way. You cannot receive your full blessing from God until you say, "Lord, I forgive them despite what they said and what they did. I forgive them and ask you to bless them." A lot of us are in the shape we're in because we won't let go of the past.

This woman who had been bent over for eighteen years found a way to press through the crowd, hoping Jesus would see her condition. When Jesus looked at this woman, He looked pass her physical ailment and saw her condition. A lot of us come to the church camouflaged. We do not want anyone to know we have issues. We may be in the midst of a storm, but we have to play it cool and not let anyone know that we are hurting. The pastor's message may bless you, but you will not show the emotions you are feeling because you have to maintain your dignity and your coolness. You have to keep yourself together. And while you are busy keeping it all together, God is passing by you.

God is looking for some people who don't mind showing their emotions. He is looking for people who will say, "God, I ain't all that and a bag of chips. I don't have it going on, and I don't have it all together. Lord, I'm coming to You so I can get fixed."

Did you know the church is a hospital? You have to understand a hospital is just a place for people who are sick. In a hospital, you are placed in different areas depending on your condition. Some people need to be monitored twenty-four hours a day because they need serious attention while others do not need to be watched as closely. Some people can share a room while others need to be in isolation. When you enter the house of the Lord, tell God, "Lord, I need You to take me to ICU! I need intensive care. I need You watching me, keeping me, and protecting me every step of the way, Lord. I'm in an ICU situation, and I can't make it without you. I've discovered I'll fail without You in my life."

This woman was in the right place. She didn't look as good as the rest of the people, but it did not matter because God chooses the brokenhearted over church folk. Jesus noticed her because she was downtrodden. He didn't choose the sanctified church member, the one who claimed to have it all together. He chose the person who admitted she had a problem. Jesus specializes in folk who have problems.

If you had it together, you would not need God. If you knew everything, you would be God! If you have it all together, it is best you stay home because the church is for messed up people who have been lied on, despised, used, and manipulated. The church is for people who have issues that only God can solve.

Do you realize that God blesses people who admit they can't do it by themselves? Do you know God uses the people the world does not want? God uses people who admit their need for Him. God uses people who are messed up. God took a murderer named Moses who was running for his life, fixed him and sent him to go back to the same place where he committed the crime to lead His people out of bondage. God took a man named Jacob—a liar, deceiver, and back-stabber—and wrestled with him until He said, "Jacob, I've forgotten your past. I've forgotten what you said and what you've done. I'm only focused on your today and your tomorrow." Jacob wrestled with God and God won. God used a prostitute named Rahab to hide His children. He took another prostitute, Mary Magdalene, and made her His faithful servant. He took Lot and let his two daughters sleep with him so that Moab was conceived, a child who was the ancestor of a woman named Ruth. God used Ruth, a widow living in a foreign land to bring forth the lineage of King David, to which Jesus was born. If you have issues, then you are one of the people God uses. He takes people who have admitted their problems and changes the situation.

Jesus looked at this woman in the crowd and said, "Come forward." Why would Jesus bring her forward? Jesus was not embarrassing her. He wanted to see how desperate she was. She had been in this state for eighteen years. The problem was her own doing. She had allowed what others said about her to affect her life. Notice that Jesus did not offer healing; nor did He suggest counseling. He knew all she needed was a word. Jesus told the woman, "I can't bless you until I release you from your past." She was not sick, so Jesus did not say, "By your faith you are healed." He didn't need to say that. Instead He said, *"Woman, thou art loosed from thine infirmity"* (Luke 13:12).

God is telling you, "I cannot inhale you until you exhale." Jesus said, *"No man, having put his hand to the plough, and looking back, is fit for the kingdom of God"* (Luke 9:62). Paul said, *"Forgetting those things which are behind, and reaching forth unto those things which are before"* (Philippians 3:13). You cannot change what you did to people. You cannot change what they did to you. So forget the past and press toward the mark. Too many Christians are still living in yesterday. You have to get out of your past so God can deal with your circumstances. God cannot bless you until you are loosed from whatever and whoever messed you up. Jesus said, *"But if ye forgive not men their trespasses, neither will your Father forgive your trespasses"* (Matthew 6:15). In other words, Jesus is saying, "I can't even forgive you until you have forgiven those who have hurt you." As a result, we have brought a lot of our problems from our past into our present. If you will let go of the past, Jesus will speak a Word over your life right now. He will speak a Word of deliverance, health, healing, wellness, and prosperity. He will speak a house, a husband, a car, a job—whatever you need. Jesus will remove everything that has been hindering you and speak blessings from God.

The devil no longer reigns over your life. He can no longer keep you stuck in yesterday. If you can receive that, then give God your best praise right now. When you give God your best praise, you have to start acting like you have been delivered. You have to start acting like you have been set free. You have to start acting like God is God and He can do whatever He says He can do. You have to change your mindset. It is your mind you have to renew.

Jesus brought the woman forward, touched her, and made her stand in front of the crowd. Why would he make her stand in front of the crowd? Because He wanted her to be able to stand when the wind tried to knock her down. The same people who had talked about her watched her come forward. Jesus knew people were going to lie on her and laugh at her. He knew they would talk about her again. She needed to know that she was standing because of the grace of God. It was His mercy and forgiveness that let her stand up straight.

Stop talking about your past. Stop bringing up what somebody did to you. That's why you are in the shape you're in! Stop talking about being a single parent and how you can't make it because you are only one parent with three kids. The devil is a liar! You serve a God who can give you an overflow. You don't need anyone else to complete you. The moment you accepted Christ as Lord, God completed you. He will give you your heart's desire. Quit making excuses for why you're in your current condition. Stop saying, "God, I made my bed, and I'm going to sleep in it."

Instead, tell God, "Lord, I'm going to worship my way out of this mess. I'm not making excuses any longer." Every time you make an excuse for the shape you are in, the devil is the only one who gets the glory. God never brings you *through* something without taking you *to* something. Luke 13:13 says that when Jesus delivered this woman from her past, she praised and glorified God.

God is no longer in yesterday. He does not deal with people who operate in yesterday. How do I know? His Word says, *"Let the dead bury their dead" (Luke 9:60).* In 1 Samuel 3, God stopped speaking to Eli, and Eli did not receive any more visions. Eli represented tradition. God stopped speaking to Eli, but He started speaking to Samuel. Samuel represented a new direction.

That's why you are not growing in your relationship with God. You are stuck in yesterday. God is saying, "I'm the same God, but I'm not speaking that way anymore." You are still waiting on God, still reading the book, *Who Moved My Cheese?* God is still blessing, but you must realize that your cheese has been moved. You cannot remain stuck in yesterday. Do not limit God. Do not box Him in. If you are ever going to receive your full blessing from God, you have to let go of your past.

This woman suffered with infirmities for eighteen years, but she stole the scene because her desperation was in her very presence. If you are going to be a scene stealer, let go of your past, speak God's Word over your life, and then lift up your hands to give God the best praise you can.

Scene Three Review

1. What is one reason many people are in the shape they are in?

2. Complete the following statement: "Jesus specializes in folk who have..."

3. List three scene stealers who were identified in the Old Testament and describe their circumstances.

4. What helped the woman stand in front of the crowd?

5. What must you do to receive your full blessing from God?

Suggested answers to these questions are on page 69.

Scene stealers do not worry about what people may think about them. They do not worry that the people sitting behind them can't see. They have been delivered from church folk, so they don't care what people think. A scene stealer will say, "I've got some issues, and I've got to get this off my chest. Father forgive me because I'm about to act like a fool."

Scene 4

The Woman With an Issue of Blood

And a certain woman, which had an issue of blood twelve years, And had suffered many things of many physicians, and had spent all that she had, and was nothing bettered, but rather grew worse, When she had heard of Jesus, came in the press behind, and touched his garment. For she said, If I may touch but his clothes, I shall be whole (Mark 5:25–28).

This scene stealer had been bleeding for twelve years. Leviticus 15:25–27 gives us a glimpse of the ordeal this woman had suffered.

"And if a woman have an issue of her blood many days out of the time of her separation (menstruation), or if it run

*beyond the time of her separation
(menstruation); all the days of the issue
of her uncleanness shall be as the days
of her separation (menstruation): she
shall be unclean. Every bed whereon
she lieth all the days of her issue shall
be unto her as the bed of her separation
(menstruation): and whatsoever she
sitteth upon shall be unclean, as the
uncleanness of her separation (menstruation). And whosoever toucheth those
things shall be unclean, and shall wash
his clothes, and bathe himself in water,
and be unclean until the even."*

Most women experience a menstrual cycle of three
to seven days. Some may also experience the excruci-
ating pain of cramps. This woman had been menstruating for twelve years. Imagine how bad you may feel
for two or three days out of a month. Now, think about
how she must have felt for twelve years. That is 144
months, 624 weeks, 4,380 days, 105,120 hours,
6,307,200 minutes, and 378,432,000 seconds—twelve
long years.

The author of Mark wasn't even writing about her.
The author was writing about Jarius, a ruler of the
synagogue whose daughter lay dying. Jesus was on His
way to heal Jairus' daughter. The author didn't even
call her by name. He called her by her condition. You
know how we call people by their condition, e.g., the

wine-o on the corner, the homeless man at the bus stop, the blind piano man. That is how we recognize them. The author identified this woman as "the woman who had the issue of blood for twelve years."

Whatever your condition, do not let it dictate where you want to be when God is finished with you. No matter what they call you, it does not mean you have to be what they say. Jabez said, "Mama, I know you were going through some stuff when I was born, but I refuse to be called pain. When I look at myself in the mirror, I see myself expanding my coast and widening my territory. I refuse to let what you call me define who I am."

Mark 5:26 says, *"And had suffered many things of many physicians, and had spent all that she had, and was nothing bettered, but rather grew worse."* She had spent all her money going to every expert in the medical field. Each of them had an opinion. Each of them tried to put her on medication and give her injections, but none of them could stop the bleeding. She could not be cured because what she had was incurable by man.

When she heard about Jesus, she did not hesitate. She immediately pressed through the crowd to touch His garment. Only when you get to the point of brokenness will you worship with your whole heart.

I can recognize people who have gone through some difficulties recently in their lives because their worship suddenly increases. The people around do not know what you have been dealing with, but they can clearly see that you worship as if you have lost yourself in God.

Scene stealers do not worry about what people may think about them. They do not worry that the people sitting behind them can't see. They have been delivered from church folk, so they don't care what people think. A scene stealer will say, "I've got some issues, and I've got to get this off my chest. Father forgive me because I'm about to act like a fool."

The woman heard that Jesus was walking down the street. She did not try to schedule an appointment because a scene stealer will burst through the crowd and let Him know she is desperate for Him. You have to understand how a scene stealer behaves.

She understood the law of Leviticus. She knew that if she touched somebody, she would defile the person. When you are desperate—have lost all of your money, gone to every doctor, and you are still sick— you are not concerned about anyone else. Your mind is saying, "It's about me right now. Lord, I need a breakthrough."

She told herself, "If I can just get through the crowd and touch the hem of His garment, I will be made whole." Why did she want to touch the hem? The hem of the garment was where the authority was. She did not just show up by coincidence. She had a plan of action.

Psalm 133:2 says:

> *It is like the precious ointment [or anointing] upon the head, that ran down upon the beard, even Aaron's beard: that went down to the skirts [the hem] of his garments.*

During biblical times, they wore long robes so the hem was almost to the ground, which meant she had to get on her knees. If you want to steal the scene and direct all of God's attention to you, you have to be willing to get on your knees.

This woman did not just show up. She understood that she was there for her breakthrough. She knew she was coming for God to open up her life and pour out a blessing. Remember Hebrews 11:6 says, *"But without faith it is impossible to please him."* She knew who she was going to see, and she believed He could heal her. You have to know who you are seeking and believe that God is God.

Recently, we took our car to the dealership for repair. We expected to pay a lot of money for the service. When we got ready to pay the cashier, the service manager said, "Mr. Hawkins, let me see if you still have a warranty on your vehicle." After checking the warranty on my vehicle, he said, "Mr. Hawkins, here are your keys. You don't have to pay anything."

Some of you need to open your Bibles to see if your warranty has expired. You may be worried that you have not been faithful at church. You have not been active in the ministry and you have not been tithing. You have not been giving God your best, so you may be concerned that your warranty has expired. You need to open your warranty manual and read Matthew 11:28, which says, *"Come unto me, all ye that labour and are heavy laden, and I will give you rest."* Then you need to read on a little further to where it says:

> *Take my yoke upon you, and learn of me; for I am meek and lowly in heart: and ye shall find rest unto your souls. For my yoke is easy, and my burden is light (Matthew 11:29–30).*

Don't stop there. Keep reading. Psalm 37:25 says, *"I have been young, and now am old; yet have I not seen the righteous forsaken, nor his seed begging bread."* Then read the final clause, which says, *"My grace is sufficient for thee"* (2 Corinthians 12:9). The price has been paid.

Your warranty will never expire. If you need a blessing and a breakthrough from God you need to know that His grace is sufficient.

This woman knew that if she touched anyone, she would make them unclean, but she was desperate. She was in pain, weak, and tired. There were men walking with Jesus, and this woman got down on her knees in the midst of a crowd. She understood where the authority of His anointing was. She thought, "I'll ask God for forgiveness later, but right now I need to touch the hem of His garment. If I can just touch the hem of His garment, I will be made whole." Her faith was in the hem.

Jesus was surrounded by people. Other people were touching Him, but they did not understand where the anointing was. When she touched His hem, Jesus felt the virtue leave His body. He stopped and asked, "Who touched me?" She tried to hide. She did not want anyone to know she had touched Him. She was really trying to get a private blessing.

Some of you have not gotten a breakthrough because you are trying to get a private praise. Jesus said, "No! Now that you have gotten your blessing, it's not about you anymore." He wants you to praise Him publicly so someone else can see your worship. Some of you don't want anyone to know that you were a whoremonger. You don't want anyone to know what you have been doing. You are trying to hide, but you must give a public testimony. You have to tell some-body else where God has brought you from.

Jesus asked, "Who touched me?" The woman finally came forward and said, "Lord, I touched you." Why did Jesus insist she come forward? It was not for her. Remember Jarius was waiting for Jesus to heal his daughter. Do you know when you hear someone's testimony and praise it benefits others? When they hear what God has done for you, they begin to believe that He will make a way for them, too.

She had to publicly tell what she was trying to hide privately. You will have to open your mouth and reveal the blessings God gives you. Has God done something that you thought could not be done? Has God opened a door for you that you thought was closed? Why are you trying to keep it quiet? If you want to be a scene stealer, if you want to get God's attention, you have to be willing to tell others how good He has been to you.

Remember, scene stealers do not fear embarrassment or condemnation. They desperately seek God and give Him their best praise.

Scene Four Review

1. Why was the name of the woman in Mark 5:25–28 not given?

2. Why was the woman forced to live in isolation?

3. Why did the woman want to touch the hem of Jesus' garmet?

4. What happened after the woman touched the hem of Jesus' garment?

5. What is the importance of your giving a testmony to others?

Suggested answers to these questions are on page 70.

You will never be a scene stealer just sitting by. Scene stealers recognize that it was not the sun nor the alarm clock that woke them up this morning. It was God. Scene stealers sit at the feet of Jesus because they expect something to happen that will transform their lives.

Scene 5

The Paraplegic Man

And it came to pass on a certain day, as he was teaching, that there were Pharisees and doctors of the law sitting by, which were come out of every town of Galilee, and Judaea, and Jerusalem: and the power of the Lord was present to heal them. And, behold, men brought in a bed a man which was taken with a palsy [a paraplegic, paralyzed]: and they sought means to bring him in, and to lay him before him. And when they could not find by what way they might bring him in because of the multitude, they went upon the housetop, and let him down through the tiling with his couch into the midst before Jesus. And when he saw their faith, he said unto

> *him, Man, thy sins are forgiven thee*
> *(Luke 5:17–20).*

The day is emphasized in this Scripture because this is the day that Jesus began teaching on days other than the Sabbath. The Jewish Sabbath was Saturday. We worship on Sunday because Jesus rose on Resurrection Sunday.

The Pharisees and lawyers were watching. They were not there to sit at Jesus' feet. They were only there out of curiosity. Whenever you come to the house of God out of curiosity, you are not really coming to sit at the feet of Christ. You are not really trying to receive God's Word. You are not trying to get delivered. You are not really trying to receive a blessing. You are there to observe.

You will never be a scene stealer just sitting by. Scene stealers recognize that it was not the sun nor the alarm clock that woke them up this morning. It was God. Scene stealers sit at the feet of Jesus because they expect something to happen that will transform their lives.

These people who were sitting by watching Jesus were the prideful, sophisticated folks. They were not broken. They were educated. They were too cool, too cute, and too rich to praise God. God is looking for people who have been broken. He wants people who have gone through hell and have come back to tell others how good God is. If you want to be a scene stealer and truly worship God, tell God, "I came to be at Your feet because I'm looking for You to do a miracle in my life."

The Pharisees and lawyers were watching while the power of the Lord was present to heal them. The presence of the Lord was right before them and the crowd did not recognize that God could have healed them. Luke 5:18 says, *"Behold..."* When we see "behold" in the Bible, that means something is about to happen suddenly. Four men brought this paralyzed man to Jesus on a stretcher. They tried to get through the crowd, but could not get in. They tried to go through the front door, the front door was crowded. They tried to go through the back door, but it was crowded too. They even tried to go through a window, but people were huddled around the windows looking in at Jesus. These men believed that if they could just get their friend next to Jesus, he would be healed. Finally, they went up on the roof to lower the man's stretcher down with a rope. They tore a hole in another man's roof!

Scene stealers will use any means necessary to get to God. Scene Stealers don't have time for people who are playing games. They are serious about God.

They lowered the paralyzed man, and when Jesus saw their faith, He said, *"Man, thy sins are forgiven thee."* Wait a minute! Jesus saw *their* faith. The paralyzed man's sins were forgiven, not because of his faith, but because of the faith of his four friends.

Do you realize that God will bless you just because of your associates? You need to make sure you are connected with some scene stealers. You need to be praying with people who are just as desperate to get to God as you (are).

Likewise, if you are a scene stealer, the people who are with you are going to be blessed just because they are standing beside you. That means I can bring somebody with me to church, and if I worship hard enough, God will forgive their sins based on my praise. That's a reason to shout! When you give God your best praise, He will not only bless you, He will also bless the people around you. Call your best friends and tell them, "Come worship with me. You don't have to do anything. Your life is about to change just because you are next to me. All you have to do is show up. I'm about to overflow your life." Because of your faith, your loved ones can be forgiven. Because of your faith, they can receive their healing. Because of your faith they can be delivered.

This is why it is so important for you to be around some battle-tested saints. You may have some people in your circle of friends who are quiet and solemn, but everyone in your circle cannot be that way. You need to find somebody who will represent you. Husbands, if your wife will not worship, you still give God your best praise. Wives, if your husband will not raise his hands, you raise both of yours and give God the praise He is due. Don't worry about whether your spouse praises

God or not. Look at them and say, "Baby, you can sit down if you want. I've got enough energy to praise God for both of us! I'll worship for both of us when we get to church!"

I believe these four men had read the story of the Hebrew boys—Shadrach, Meshach, and Abednego—in the fiery furnace (Daniel 3:8–30). These men believed that if God could bring those three Hebrew boys out of the fiery furnace and take the smoke from their clothes, then *surely* God could heal their friend.

Notice that Jesus cleansed the man before He healed him. The healing was about to come, but Jesus made sure He removed all of the impurities first. God wants you to know that He healed you and no one else. He wants you to know that He blessed you. God is the one who set you free.

Jesus forgave the man of his sins, and then told him to arise and walk. The man stood up, picked up his stretcher, and went home praising God. This man received his blessing because of four courageous, faith-walking, bold, God-fearing scene stealers. The presence of the Lord was there to heal, but only these men who climbed the roof stole His attention. The only person Jesus blessed was the paraplegic. If you want your breakthrough, you have to learn how to steal a scene, and give God the best praise you can.

Scene Five Review

1. Why is *"a certain day"* emphasized in Luke 5:17?

2. Why were the Pharisees and lawyers watching (sitting by)?

3. Why do scene stealers sit at the feet of Jesus?

4. What does *behold* in the Bible mean?

5. Who did Jesus bless in Luke 5:24–25?

Suggested answers to the questions are on page 70.

Conclusion

Throughout this book, I described the characteristics of a scene stealer and showed you biblical characters as examples. Now, I would like to introduce you to a couple of modern day scene stealers. The first one is my wife, Debbie.

Some years ago, Debbie sought employment at a very well known small business in Atlanta. After her interview, the owner of the company said he was going to hire her and that he would contact her within a week. A week went by and my wife had not received a call. As she began approaching the second week, she became desperate. She prayed to God, reminding Him that this job was hers and the owner had promised her the job.

Now, you have to know my five-foot-three-refuse-to-accept-no-for-an-answer wife. The following Monday morning, she rose early with expectancy. After her morning prayer, she put on her business suit, dropped the kids off at school and daycare, and went to work. Upon her arrival, all of the other spectators (employees), were looking and whispering. The owner of the company finally arrived and my wife explained that she was there to report to work. Since he had stated that he would contact her, she was afraid that he may have misplaced her telephone number or tried to call and she missed his telephone call. Nevertheless, she was there and ready to report to work. The owner was so furious (actually outdone) that he told her to go sit in a cubicle and he would get to her later.

Ten years passed and Debbie became one of that company's greatest assets. She became his project manager and his personal spiritual advisor. She remained faithful to his company until God moved her into a full-time position in the ministry. Debbie had a prayer in her heart and a fight in her spirit to go after what God had shown and promised her. My wife does not believe in pity parties. She speaks to ladies around the world in seminar settings, encouraging them to go after the things of God.

Just recently, God impressed upon her heart to go back to college. She contacted the college. They told her that she was a couple of days too late to register for the current semester. Again, this scene stealer refused to accept no for an answer. Debbie doesn't operate out of arrogance, but assurance and humility. She decided to drive to the school with expectancy.

Debbie could have accepted what they told her and waited to start the next semester; however, she knew she was supposed to start right away. Debbie's mindset was, "If I can just get to the school." In other words, she knew she had to get to the right place and in the right position. She never disclosed who she was, but spoke with someone in the admissions office. God allowed another woman to overhear her conversation. This woman stepped into the midst of a *no* and said *yes*. My wife is currently enrolled in school.

I am proud to write that I am a scene stealer. God called me to start Voices of Faith Ministries in 1994. I had no money and was without a place to worship. My only members were my wife and kids. But I knew God had given me a vision so I started Bible study in my home. I rented a recreation building and began Sunday morning worship service. After a few months, I found an interim location. This church was going to allow us to worship a few hours prior to their service.

On the first Sunday, God packed the house, and the pastor told me I could only use his building for one more Sunday and I had to go. We returned to the recreation center and remained there for about a year. We eventually found another church to hold our services. We held 7:30 a.m. services for almost two years until again (due to phenomenal growth), we were asked to leave.

I could have easily given up, but God showed favor and allowed us to find a location the same week. A school opened their doors to us. God began to speak to me. I was trying to put new wine in an old wine bottle. I was looking for an existing church, but God wanted me to build. I became very frustrated, but every day I got up and pursued land. One day, while driving God told me to pull over, and as I got out of the vehicle, He said, "Be careful for you are standing on holy ground. This is the place where I want you to build." I began to weep and praise God on the land. There were many trees. I cannot tell you the countless times I passed this location. I was looking for a "For Sale" sign, but the land was not for sale. God allowed me to locate the owners, who were not even residents of Georgia. I shared my vision with the owner and God gave us the land.

Currently, we own nine buildings, which include a youth sanctuary (our first church), family life center, activity center, outreach center, daycare, academy, gymnasium with softball field, teen house, and our newly built church for our second location in Conyers, Georgia.

What makes me a scene stealer? Each time God told me to pursue land to build upon or to purchase an existing structure, I did not have the money to buy it. I believed that if God showed it to me, then I could believe Him for it. I believed, and I spoke it. I believe and I speak it (2 Corinthians 4:13).

One thing that hinders our prayers is that we ask and pray, but we do not believe we deserve what we just asked for. We don't share our vision because we don't want egg on our faces if it doesn't manifest. But the Bible tells us in the Book of Romans, *"to speak those things that be not as though they were" (Romans 4:17).*

God knows that I am kingdom-minded. I share with others how God did it for me. If He did it for me, He will certainly do it for you. God is no respecter of person.

I pray that after reading this book, you will pursue life differently. You should have a mind that's willing to share with others when pursuing the things of God. Remember, church thinking is "I got mine, so you have to figure out how to get yours." Kingdom-thinking is "God healed me, and I will not rest until I share with someone how to be healed." May God transform your heart into one of a true worshipper. May He give you the boldness to do whatever it takes to always get His attention.

Gary Hawkins, Sr.

Answers to Review Question

Scene One Answers

1. It refers to how knowledge of the miracles Jesus had performed was spreading by word of mouth.

2. The two blind men
   The woman with the issue of blood
   Blind Bartimaeus

3. Their incredible faith caused them to be healed.

4. They are never embarassed to do whatever it takes to get God's attention. They give God continual praise. They always operate on their own behalf. They are desperate. They do not care about what other people think of them.

5. We do not pray specifically with faith.

Scene Two Answers

1. To do all they can to have God's attention rest upon them.

2. a. He positioned himself to see Jesus.
   b. He refused to let the people stop him.

c. He was willing to cast off his garment (any
dead weight in his life.)

3. He asked for mercy.

4. The devil will try to prevent you from receiving
what God wants to give you.

5. Bartimaeus cast off his garment. He got rid of the
dead weight in his life.

Scene Three Answers

1. Because they will not let go of their past. They are
stuck in yesterday.

2. problems

3. Examples are:
a. Moses: murderer, fugitive, led the Israelites out
of Egypt
b. Jacob: liar, deceiver, backstabber, wrestled
with God
c. Rahab: prostitute:, hid and protected the men
who went to spy out the Promised Land

4. The grace, mercy, and forgiveness of God.

5. You must let go of your past.

Scene Four Answers

1. She was called by her condition, "a certain woman who had an issue of blood for twelve years."

2. A woman was considered unclean when she was menstruating. Anyone she touched during that time would be defiled.

3. The authority was in the hem of the garment.

4. Jesus felt the virtue leave His body. He stopped and asked, "Who touched me?"

5. Your testimony will benefit others.

Scene Five Answers

1. It is when Jesus began teaching on days other than the Sabbath.

2. They were curious.

3. Because they expect something to happen that will transform their lives.

4. It means that something is about to happen suddenly.

5. The paraplegic man

ORDER FORM
Order by phone, fax, mail, or online

Gary Hawkins Ministries   Phone: 770-498-5850
P. O. Box 870989   Fax: 770-498-1566
Stone Mountain, GA 30087   www.voicesfaith.org

QTY	ITEM	EACH	TOTAL
	Marketing Your Church for Growth – Book	$ 12.95	
	Marketing Your Church for Growth – Audio Cassette	10.95	
	Marketing Your Church for Growth – CD	15.95	
	Fighting for Your Destiny – Book	13.95	
	God's Best for Your Life	15.95	
	Marketing Through Faith – Home Work Study	50.00	
	Eight Steps to Prosperity	15.95	
	What Every Pastor Should Know	14.95	
	Marketing for Next Level Ministry – Book	15.95	
	From the Heart of First Ladies	15.95	
	What Every First Lady Should Know	14.95	
	COMING SOON:		
	When Faith Meets Promise		
	Marketing for the Next Dimension		
	Subtotal	$	
	Postage and Handling (Call for Shipping Charges)	$	
	Total	$	

Name _____ Date _____

Address _____ Apt./Unit _____

City_____ State_____Zip _____

Payment Method: ☐ VISA ☐ MC ☐ AMEX ☐ Discover ☐ Check

Credit Card #_____ Exp. _____

Signature _____

ABOUT THE AUTHOR

Gary Hawkins, Sr. is a graduate of Luther Rice Seminary in Lithonia, Georgia. He is the founding pastor of Voices of Faith Ministries in Stone Mountain and Conyers, Georgia. Voices of Faith has seen its membership grow from 75 people to more than 9,000 in only seven years. It has been recognized by *Church Growth Magazine* as the 25th fastest growing church in America. Gary Hawkins, Sr. was recognized by *The Church Report* magazine as one of the top twenty-five leaders to watch in 2005 and listed in Strathmore's Who's Who in September 2006. Gary and his wife, Debbie, live in Loganville, Georgia with their four children, Elaina, Ashley, Gary Jr., and Kalen.